THE *Empowered* EXECUTOR

Executor's Survival Guide

A Holistic Approach for Canadian Families

SHELLEY ESSERY

Disclaimer

All guidance provided by The Empowered Executor is for informational purposes only. Our services are intended to offer general advice and information and should not be construed as professional advice.

The Empowered Executor does not guarantee the accuracy, completeness, or suitability of the information provided. Users should consult with appropriate professionals for specific advice tailored to their individual situations.

The use of any information provided by The Empowered Executor is solely at the user's own risk and The Empowered Executor shall not be held liable for any direct or indirect damages arising from the use of our services or reliance on the information provided.

Table of Contents

Foreword

The Executor's Survival Guide: A Holistic Approach for Canadian Families leads families and executors on a compassionate path towards estate administration, allowing them to work together to ensure that the needs of the executor, the departed, & the family are being cared for. This practical, easy to understand resource prioritizes the relationship between the departed, their loved ones, and their executor. It includes suggestions for how to have difficult conversations, offers strategies for self-care, and provides suggestions for grief support throughout the process of estate administration.

When families & loved ones share a respect for the executor's role and have a clear understanding of the executor's duties, the executor is able to navigate their role with confidence. This allows the family to trust that their loved one's legacy is truly being honoured.

In both my role as a Wills & Estates Legal Administrator and as the Co-Founder of The Empowered Estate, I have witnessed the breakdown of family relationships after death. This is often because of anger or hurt feelings stemming from poorly set expectations. When there is a lack of communication between the family and the executor, both parties are forced to fill in the blanks with assumptions. And when there is a lack of knowledge and understanding of the estate administration process, the confusion can lead to conflict.

I have seen the disappointment in a parent's face when a child refuses to accept the role of executor, simply because they lack knowledge and confidence to perform the role... And I have witnessed the hurt in a child's face when a parent makes choices regarding their estate administration without communicating clearly, or without considering the lasting effects of those choices. I have listened to concerns from both will makers and executors, and most often, these concerns are rooted in unfounded fears, a lack of information, or miscommunication.

Nobody wants their death to tear their family apart. Nobody dies wanting to leave their loved ones hurt and confused- yet it happens all the time. This guide was written to provide the will maker, the family, and the executor with a basic understanding of the process of estate administration and the duties of an executor. When a will maker understands the executor's role, they can better set their executor up for success. Similarly, when a family understands the executor's role, they can better understand their own rights and entitlements throughout the process. Finally, when an executor understands their own role, they can navigate it with confidence while ensuring that they are also meeting the needs of the family.

In my experience, an informed family is an emotionally well-equipped family. Navigating the handling of a loved one's estate from a place of compassion leads to peace of mind for everyone.

With some basic shared information, a general understanding of the executor role, and clear communication, the estate administration process can be managed smoothly and compassionately.

The information shared in this guide, while directed towards the executor, is intended for everyone. Will makers will better understand the importance of providing their executor with as much direction & access to information as possible, and family members will gain a better operational understanding of the estate administration process.

This guide demonstrates how enmeshed an executor is with the departed and their loved ones. It demonstrates how important everyone's role is, and how knowledge & communication are the keys to successfully administering an estate while maintaining positive relationships.

To the will maker, use this guide as a tool to ensure your executor is set up for success.

To the loved ones left behind, use this guide as a tool to understand the role of executor, your rights, and your entitlements for access to information throughout the estate administration process.

To the executor, use this guide as a tool to understand your role, your obligations, and to facilitate communication with reluctant will makers seeking your support.

Being an executor is an honour and a privilege. You have been entrusted with someone's legacy, and your role is more than administrative. As executor, you act as a bridge.

You facilitate someone's final act of love to those they leave behind. The final chapter of their legacy is in your capable and caring hands.

Serving as executor can be emotionally and physically exhausting. It's important that you develop a plan to take care of yourself throughout your executor journey. Remember: first and foremost, you are grieving, too. Allow yourself some grace. There is nothing more important than your health and safety. Your loved one wouldn't want the role of executor to negatively impact your physical or mental well-being. Take care of yourself first, then take care of the estate.

When it comes to estate administration, there is a solution to every challenge. As executor, it is not up to you to know all the answers. However, it is up to you to know *who to ask* for the answers. Build your support team of trusted professionals, then work with them to confidently administer the estate. Support is always available and with the right assistance, the administration process will be easier to navigate.

I've worked with many executors who feel stressed because they're unsure of how to be effective in the executor role. They don't know about all of the tasks that need to be accomplished and worry about making mistakes. In an effort to be mindful of how much money the estate is spending on legal fees, an executor may hesitate to ask questions or seek direction when necessary. While not intentional, this results in a more complicated administration process for everyone. Knowledge is power, and an empowered executor is a more efficient executor. Efficient executors help save the estate money and administer it more quickly, more smoothly, and with fewer complications.

This organizer will guide you through the typical order and basic steps of an estate administration. While legally, you are not obligated to hire a lawyer for support in administering an estate, I recommend consulting a lawyer for advice. Each estate is unique and will present its own challenges. Asking for help when you need it makes you a better executor, not a worse one!

For your convenience, I have included sample worksheets as part of this resource. These worksheets are for personal use only; Please feel free to revise or edit as it applies to your unique situation or makes sense for your purposes.

To download full versions of these templates for personal use, go to https://www.shelleyessery.com.

Introduction

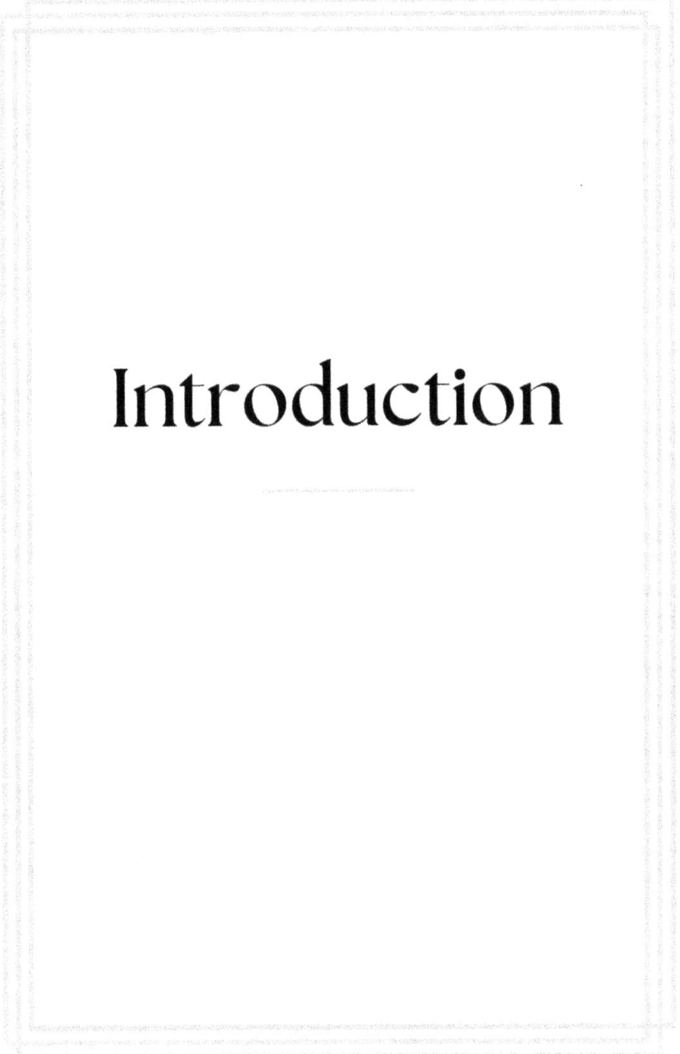

Before agreeing to be an executor, you must first understand what you are agreeing to.

EXECUTOR LIABILITY

An executor is NOT personally liable for the deceased's debts!

An executor is personally liable for ensuring proper administration of the estate to the best of their ability. This includes:

1. Determining the proper value of each asset
2. Managing or distributing them to maximize the benefit to the estate

As an executor, you are responsible for managing or selling the estate's assets for the highest possible value. If you dispose of an asset for less than its fair market value without consideration for the beneficiaries, then you should be able to justify the sale and provide evidence that you acted in good faith. Otherwise, you may be held accountable for reimbursing the estate for the difference between the sale price and its fair market value.

Ensure all proven debts have been paid in full, including any interest, penalties, or taxes owing.

As an executor, you can be held personally liable if you distribute funds to beneficiaries before settling all of the estate's debts. If you distribute funds to beneficiaries, and it is later determined that the estate owes more money than the remaining assets are able to cover, then you could be held responsible for paying any remaining debts out of your own pocket.

<u>TIP</u>: Get a Clearance Certificate!

Before making the final distribution to the beneficiaries, you should apply to the CRA for a

Clearance Certificate to confirm that all income tax and GST/HST (if applicable) due has been paid in full. Once you have received a Clearance Certificate, you can no longer be held personally responsible for unpaid taxes.

Before submitting your application, be sure you have completed the following:

a) You have filed all necessary tax returns and received Notices of Assessment for each return.

b) All monies owing to the CRA have been paid in full, including adjustments for interest, penalty, taxpayer relief, or appeal requests.

EXECUTOR COMPENSATION

As executor, you may choose to collect Executor's Compensation. In Canada, Executor's Compensation is typically between 3%-5%. This is charged in accordance with provincial rules, or as set out in the will. Note that **Executor's Compensation is considered taxable income and must be reported as income on your tax return.**

*Co-Executors: If there are one or more co-executors, the executor's compensation will be split.

Chapter 1

The Role of Executor

What is an Executor?

An executor – also referred to as an executrix, administrator, or estate trustee – is the person responsible for administering the estate in accordance with the terms of the will. In cases where no will has been created, then they are tasked with administering the estate in accordance with provincial laws.

An executor assumes full responsibility for the management of all assets and debts of the deceased. It is the job of the executor to ensure that all legal paperwork has been completed, all taxes have been filed & paid, all debts have been settled, and all assets have been distributed in accordance with the terms of the will or provincial laws.

What are the Risks of being an Executor?

The role of executor can carry personal financial risk. An executor can be sued if they fail to properly protect or manage assets, follow the terms of the will, or if they engage in illegal activity in connection with the executor role.

If an executor distributes assets of the estate without ensuring all debts have been paid, the executor can be held personally liable for payment of those outstanding debts.

What is Executor's Compensation?

An executor is entitled to financial compensation for administering the estate. The compensation amount is typically based on a percentage of the value of the estate.

Can I Refuse to be an Executor?

Even if you have been named as an executor in a will, you have the right to decline the role. If you have not handled any of the estate's assets and you do not wish to be the executor, you will need to sign a formal Notice of Renunciation as soon as possible. This form will be filed with the court when someone else applies to be appointed to administer the estate.

What is Executor's Liability Insurance?

Executor's liability insurance is relatively new and worth looking into – particularly if you are dealing with a complex estate or if there are contentious family dynamics in play.

Executor's liability insurance can provide protection from liability arising from inadvertent negligent administration of the estate. It will help cover your costs to defend your actions in court and payment of damages in the event of a judgment against you.

Executor liability insurance won't typically cover foreign or business assets, unpaid taxes, failure to maintain proper insurance coverage on estate assets, fraud, dishonesty, malicious activity, or illegal activity within your role as executor.

Chapter 2

Getting Started

Immediate Actions

1. Locate the Will

If you have agreed to be the executor for the estate, the first thing you need to do is locate & review the most recent and original **ink-signed** will. Once located, **DO NOT** give out the original will. The court requires the original document to apply for probate.

Currently, British Columbia is the only province in Canada that accepts a will that has been signed electronically. To prove its validity, you may be asked for a digital security trace, security certificate, and/or a copy of the video recording taken when the deceased completed the digital signature.

Once you have the original will in your possession, you are allowed to make photocopies for the purpose of administering the estate.

However, a simple photocopy isn't always sufficient – particularly for tasks related to handling money or other assets. It's likely that you will be asked to provide a notarized copy.

A notarized document simply means that a notary has compared the photocopy to the original and attached their certificate stating that the photocopy is a true copy of the original document. A Notary will usually charge a fee for this service.

If no will can be found, check with the Canada Will Registry to inquire if one was registered: https://canadawillregistry.org/

If you are the executor for someone who has passed away without a will (in cases like this, the deceased is referred to as an "intestate"), you will need to apply to the court to be appointed as the estate administrator. Usually, the spouse of the deceased is given the highest priority for this role, followed by the deceased's children. In the case of an intestacy, you will need to follow provincial rules for administering the estate.

2. <u>Codicil</u>

A codicil is a legal document, signed in the same manner as a will. It makes a specific modification to a will after it is signed. Most often, a codicil is used to change the name of an executor. However, it can also be used to make other changes to the original terms of the will. If there is a codicil to the will, the modification it contains supersedes the original statement in the will. For example, if the codicil names a new executor, then that individual is now the legal executor of the will, rather than the person initially named executor in the will.

3. <u>Memorandum or Bequests</u>

A memorandum or list of bequests is simply a list of personal wishes for how the deceased would prefer their personal items (such as jewellery, art, or even memorial arrangements) to be handled. It is not a legally binding document. As executor, it is up to you to use your best judgment on the disposition of these items. It is preferable to distribute the personal items in accordance with the deceased's wishes, to the best of your ability.

4. <u>Review of Testamentary Documents</u>

Contrary to what is seen on TV, there is no "Reading of the Will".

Once you have gathered all of the testamentary documents, carefully review the terms of the will and any changes that may have been made by a codicil. Determine who the beneficiaries are and what they receive from the estate. A beneficiary may be gifted a specific gift, amount of money, or receive a share of the residue of the estate.

The residue of the estate is what's left after all the assets have been liquidated and all the debts, including taxes, professional fees, and executor's compensation have been paid.
At this stage, you are simply gathering information. **Do not make any distribution of assets from the estate.**

As executor, you are legally required to keep a full accounting of all physical assets that the deceased owned at the time of death, as well as the eventual distribution of said assets.

Probate fees are based on the value of the estate; therefore, it is imperative that you take a full inventory so you can thoroughly review each item to determine its proper value.

5. <u>Funeral Arrangements</u>

If the death has just occurred, and no pre-planning is in place, you may want to refer to the deceased's memorial wishes (if any) when making the funeral arrangements. However, you are not legally obligated to honour the deceased's wishes.

A funeral director can assist you in making the final arrangements and help you obtain the death certificate. To apply for a death certificate, you will need to provide a copy of the will (if one is available) as evidence that you are the executor. You will also need to provide the following information about the deceased:

1. Full Legal Name
2. Maiden Name (if applicable)
3. Gender
4. Personal Health Number
5. Social Insurance Number
6. Date of Death

7. Place of Death

8. Date of Birth

9. Place of Birth

10. First Nations Status (if applicable) and whether they lived on a Reserve

11. Home Address

12. Occupation

13. Marital Status and (if applicable) Married & Maiden Names of the Spouse

14. Parents' Names (including Maiden names, if applicable) and Places of Birth

If you are considering posting an obituary, be mindful about what personal information you are sharing. It's becoming more common for scam artists to take advantage of families by using information found in an obituary to commit identity theft. Avoid using exact dates, full names, home addresses or places of employment.

It is the responsibility of the estate to pay for the funeral expenses. If there are no funds immediately available, and you as the executor personally pay for any costs associated with the funeral, make sure you keep all receipts to ensure that you are able to be reimbursed.

Above all else, remember that the most important thing you can do at this stage is take the time you need to honour your grief. Processing the death, being with loved ones, and mourning in whatever way you need to is vital while making the final arrangements. The legal work and your executor duties are secondary to your immediate needs.

While you are obligated to administer the estate in a timely manner, it is perfectly okay to take the time and the breaks you need to process the death. Do not feel any pressure to begin the administration process immediately.

The traditional guideline for administering an estate is to complete it within one year. However, as estates grow more complex and court backlogs delay probate, many estates take longer to settle. Many of these delays can be out of your control. As an executor, it's your responsibility to oversee the estate administration process and ensure it progresses within a reasonable timeframe **to the best of your ability**.

Chapter 3

Secure Assets & Determine Liabilities

Important Next Steps:

6. <u>Secure Assets of the Deceased</u>

There are a few tasks you should be ready to handle as soon as possible to avoid potential problems.

a) Determine and secure all assets owned by the deceased at the time of death. Create a complete list of assets and their values on date of death. For items such as art and jewellery that will be sold for the benefit of the estate, use an accredited appraiser to determine fair market value. For household contents or items of minimal value, consider hiring a professional service to provide a written opinion on the overall value. Remember to check for income that is still due to the estate, such as CPP/OAS, vacation pay, or employment bonus. For employment-related assets, contact the employer to arrange the return of the assets as soon as possible. Keep in mind that any information contained on the asset is the legal property of the company.

b) Ensure the assets are protected and/or insured where applicable.

c) If the deceased owned real estate, either as a principal residence or as a rental property, confirm that an insurance policy is in place and will be maintained until the property can be legally transferred to a new owner. Contact the insurance company to advise them of the death and inform them of whether the property is vacant or occupied. Have the property appraised by three (3) independent real estate agents for its value on the date of death. For probate purposes, you will use the average of these three evaluations.

d) You are responsible for all content located at the deceased's property. Since you have no way of knowing who has a key, you should consider changing all of the locks to ensure that you are in full control of who has access to the property. In the event that someone with a key enters the property and removes any of its contents, you can be held liable to reimburse the estate for the value of the removed items, as you failed to take the necessary steps to secure the property and contents.

e) Unplug unnecessary appliances, clean out the refrigerator, and empty the garbage.

f) Perform regular property checks to pick up mail and arrange for all necessary exterior and interior property maintenance required to keep the property in good condition. Alternatively, arrange for a property watch service to monitor on your behalf. If the property is a rental, you must also collect rent payments.

g) If the deceased owned vehicles, advise the insurance company of the death and cancel the insurance policy. The vehicle(s) should remain parked and maintained until ownership can be transferred.

h) You are responsible for caring for and re-homing any pets of the deceased.

i) If the deceased owned a business, you may also be responsible for securing the business assets. Business assets can include real estate, intellectual property, and/or proprietary information. You may also be responsible for dissolving the business or attending to its transfer in accordance with a succession plan, if one exists.

j) Contact the bank to advise them of the death and determine if a safety deposit box exists. All accounts should be frozen to avoid any unauthorized withdrawals.

k) Contact the financial advisor of the deceased for a breakdown of all investments and their value on the date of death.

l) Determine if the deceased owned assets outside of the province or country.

7. Determine Debts of the Deceased

a) Review credit card statements and cancel any automatic charges relating to subscriptions or memberships, such as streaming services or gym membership.

b) You may want to consider publishing a Notice to Creditors to notify creditors of the death and provide an opportunity for any creditors to make a claim against the estate.

c) Determine if the deceased had any outstanding mortgages, lines of credit, or credit card balances. Remember to inquire if any of the balances were insured in the event of death.

8. <u>Review Digital Assets</u>

a) Determine if the deceased had any social media or email accounts and look for a list of passwords or instructions on how the deceased wished for these accounts to be handled. If you plan on leaving a social media account open for loved ones to share memories, be mindful of the risk of identity theft and ensure that you are regularly monitoring the account for suspicious activity.

b) Determine if the deceased maintained a personal or business website.

c) Determine if the deceased held any points or monetary balances owing from rewards programs or memberships.

d) Determine if the deceased held any cryptocurrencies. You will need their private key or password to access the accounts. Currently, there is no other way to access these accounts.

Chapter 4

Get Organized

The residual beneficiaries are entitled to review all statements of account and financial transactions of the estate; therefore, it is imperative that you maintain accurate and up-to-date records of every transaction you handle on behalf of the estate. While you are responsible for protecting the interests of the estate and its beneficiaries, you are also responsible for protecting your own interests as executor. So *"Cover your Butt"*!

There are some helpful online platforms available to assist executors in their role. These platforms can help you organize the administration process and provide guidance along your journey to keep you on track. By providing your login details to your trusted professional service advisors, it allows for easy and simple communication.

9. <u>Create a Complete List of Assets</u>

Anything that has a monetary value is considered an asset; this includes investments, bank accounts, and even household items. Start by creating a comprehensive inventory list that includes columns for both fair market value on date of death and actual sale price. In addition to this, create a column for your personal notes with respect to disposition, which can include details on expenses and income related to an asset.

For bank accounts and investments included on the Complete List of Assets, I suggest keeping a separate financial record for each individual account to record money in and money out. This provides full transparency and allows you to easily provide the current running balance if requested.

<u>**NOTE:**</u> You will need to provide copies of all bank and financial statements from the institution together with receipts for all income and expenses to prove your bookkeeping.

10. <u>Create a Complete List of Debts & Liabilities</u>

Create a list of all debts and liabilities that will need to be paid and closed prior to the final distribution. This includes (but is not limited to) mortgages, credit cards, loans, taxes, household bills, and/or subscriptions.

11. <u>Executor's Expenses</u>

As executor, you are entitled to claim certain expenses related to administering the estate, such as gas & mileage, cleaning supplies, utilities, and/or funeral costs paid out of pocket. Since the estate will need to reimburse you, you may wish to create a separate statement of account for Executor's Expenses to record all expenses paid by you to be reimbursed by the estate. This is an easy way to keep an ongoing record of what the estate owes you, while facilitating full transparency in the event that you are requested to prove your expenses. Remember to keep all receipts and attach them to your statement of Executor's Expenses to prove their legitimacy.

12. Financial Statement Summary

Once you have completed a detailed list of all assets and liabilities, create a Financial Statement Summary to record balances only.

Begin by creating a section for Assets, where you can list each asset along with its current value. It may be helpful to maintain a separate list for assets excluded from probate*, as they do not form part of the value of the estate. Once you've listed all the assets, calculate the total balance.

Examples of assets excluded from probate include items that pass directly to a beneficiary. This can include bequests of personal belongings like jewelry, joint accounts, and insurance policies with designated beneficiaries.

Next, following the same format, create a separate section for Debts & Liabilities, Executor's Expenses & Compensation, Anticipated Income & Expenses, and Proposed Distribution.

13. Executor's Planner

To help you stay organized during the estate administration process, use an Executor's Planner and keep it up-to-date. This will allow you to track your progress, note due dates, and prioritize your "to-do" list for any outstanding tasks. Use the planner to record your personal time spent on estate matters, including appointments & conversations with professional service providers and beneficiaries. Keeping detailed notes will provide an easy reference for what needs to happen next.

14. <u>Notify Beneficiaries</u>

Once you have reviewed the will (or the provincial rules for estate administration, in the event of intestacy), you will need to notify all the beneficiaries.

To avoid potential conflict, I recommend providing updates & communication regarding the estate to all of the beneficiaries at the same time and in the same manner.

You will first need to determine who the beneficiaries are and what they are entitled to. Next, you will need to obtain their current mailing address and telephone number.

For beneficiaries who are to receive a specific gift, such as a piece of jewellery or a set dollar amount, consider providing them with a partial copy of the will as it relates to **their gift only**. This is a good way to offer transparency, while still maintaining the privacy of the deceased.

As executor, it is your duty to protect the privacy of the deceased. You are only required to provide a copy of the will to a residual beneficiary.

Once you have obtained contact information for **all** beneficiaries, you can notify everyone at the same time and in the same manner, and provide a full copy of the will to each residual beneficiary.

Chapter 5

Probate & Administration

15. <u>Apply for Probate</u>

Not all estates are required to go through probate. You will need to review provincial rules to determine if probate is required. Probate is simply the process of having the court approve a will as valid and formally appoint the executor.

To apply for probate, you will need to:

1. Decide if you wish to retain a lawyer for assistance

2. Determine the estimated value of the estate

3. Notify beneficiaries of your intention to apply for probate

4. Submit application to the court, including the original will, death certificate, and statement of assets valued at date of death

16. Estate Bank Account

Once you have been formally approved as the executor of the estate and have been granted a probate certificate, you should open an estate bank account as soon as possible. Opening an estate bank account will simplify your bookkeeping by allowing you to deposit income and pay expenses directly through the estate.

You can now begin liquidating assets, paying debts, and closing all other accounts. If you are considering making a partial distribution to the beneficiaries, make sure to hold back enough money to pay all outstanding debts and anticipated expenses (such as professional fees, taxes, and executor's compensation) and request each beneficiary sign a Partial Release of Indemnity/Receipt and Acknowledgement before paying out any of the interim distributions. If any of the beneficiaries require a trust to be set up, this will need to be done in advance of any distribution.

17. Change Address of the Estate

It's wise to update the address associated with all assets and liabilities to your own. This ensures that you receive all notifications, and that nothing is overlooked.

18. Liquidate Assets

You can now begin liquidating the assets, making sure that all income received is deposited into the estate bank account. **Be sure to retain documentation that verifies the actual sale price.**

a) Distribute bequests to beneficiaries that fall outside of probate, such as personal items.

b) Determine the fair market value for each asset forming a part of the residue of the estate.

Consider seeking professional advice where possible. You may need to contact a real estate agent, personal property appraiser, auctioneer, car dealership, or other expert. For large ticket items, the general rule of thumb is to get three (3) independent evaluations.

c) Contact the financial advisor for a breakdown of all investments with values determined at the date of death as well as current value, and provide instructions to liquidate & close the account.

d) Liquidate and close all other bank accounts, transferring funds to the estate bank account.

e) Ensure all obligations are met regarding the transfer of jointly owned property or accounts to the surviving owner.

f) Attend to the sale of remaining assets, ensuring you have documentation of all income and expenses related to the disposition of the asset.

g) Arrange for the disposal of household items that have no significant value.

h) Arrange for the disposition and closure of any business interests.

19. <u>Pay Debts</u>

Before making final distributions to the beneficiaries, ensure that all valid debts are fully paid and accounts are closed. This includes taxes and any ongoing expenses related to managing the estate during the administration process.

As executor, it's your responsibility to pay all valid debts. You may want to consider publishing a notice to creditors to protect against unknown claims. If a debt surfaces after the estate is closed, you could be held personally liable for payment.

20. <u>File Tax Returns</u>

When administering an estate, there are two to three basic tax returns you should be aware of. But there may be additional/optional returns or forms to consider, such as income on foreign assets. Your accountant can offer the best guidance on what's required.

a) Terminal Return: a Terminal Return is filed to report income from January 1st of the year of death up to and including the date of death. If the death occurred on or before October 31st, you must file this return by April 30th of the following year. If the date of death was in November or December, you must file within six (6) months of the date of death.

b) Trust or Final Return: a Trust Return is filed to report income earned after the date of death, such as income on investments.

c) Business Returns: if the deceased held interests in a corporation or partnership, you may need to file a separate return for business income.

21. Obtain a Clearance Certificate

After liquidating the assets, paying all debts & liabilities, and filing the necessary tax returns, you can begin wrapping up the estate. To protect yourself, it's advisable to obtain a Clearance Certificate from the CRA. This certificate confirms that all taxes have been paid and that no further amounts are owed by the estate, allowing you to proceed with the final distribution.

22. Proposed Distribution and Final Statement of Account

Once you have been cleared by the CRA, prepare a detailed final statement of accounts that summarizes all transactions related to the management of the estate, including interim distributions, anticipated final professional fees, executor's compensation, and planned final distribution. The closing balance on this statement should equal zero.

23. <u>Release by Beneficiary</u>

Prior to closing the estate and paying any final distributions to the beneficiaries, you should obtain a signed Release from each beneficiary approving the Final Statement of Accounts and releasing you from any claims they may have against you as executor for the estate.

24. <u>Final Distribution and Wrap Up</u>

Once you have received signed Releases from each beneficiary, you can proceed to pay out any final expenses in accordance with your Final Statement of Accounts, including executor's fees and the final distribution payments to the beneficiaries.

You may close the estate bank account once everything has cleared the account.

Take a deep breath – this now completes your role as executor.

Loved One's Personal Information

Full Name:

____

75

Date of Death:

____

Place of Death:

____

Date of Birth:

____

Place of Birth:

____

Gender:

____

Personal Health Number:

____

Social Insurance Number:

____

Occupation:

____

Employer(s):

____

____

Self-Employed/Business Interest:

____

____

Home Address:

____

____

Pets:

____

Parent's Name and Date & Place of Birth:

____

____

Parent's Name and Date & Place of Birth:

____

____

First Nations Status & Reserve Information:

Passport #/Expiry:

____

Driver's License #/Expiry:

____

Military Service ID:

____

Firearms Permit #:

____

List of Contacts

Priority Contacts

Priority Contacts

82

Support of Family & Friends

Support of Family & Friends

Beneficiaries - Specific Bequest

Beneficiaries - Residual Share

Beneficiaries - Residual Share

Professional Services

Professional Services

Probate & Administration Checklist

Master Checklist

- Original Last Will and Testament
- Codicil(s) to Last Will and Testament
- Memorandum or Bequests
- Memorial Arrangements
- Original Death Certificate
- Notify Government Agencies and Apply for or Cancel Government Benefits
- Contact Bank to advise of Death, Freeze Accounts, and Inquire about a Safety Deposit Box
- Review Foreign Assets
- Review Credit Cards, Mortgages, and Loan Statements *(determine if insured)*
- Consult Professionals *(Lawyer, Accountant, Financial Advisor)*
- Create a Filing System and Task List to record Deadlines and Executor Notes
- Notify Beneficiaries
- Prepare List of Assets and Liabilities as of Date of Death
- Obtain Financial Statements *(Banking and Investment)*
- Review Insurance Policies
- Prepare Probate Application *(if applicable)*
- Publish a Notice to Creditors
- Obtain Expert Appraisals for High-Value Assets
- Return Employer Assets

- Make Inquiries as to Outstanding Employment or Other Income still Owing
- Advise Insurance Company and Maintain Insurance on Assets until Disposition
- Cancel Vehicle Insurance and Arrange for Fair Market Value Appraisal
- Arrange for Care of Pets
- Change Locks and Key to Property
- Dispose of Firearms
- Unplug Appliances, Clean Fridge, Empty Garbage, Dispose of Household Contents
- Attend at Real Property or Hire a Property Watch Service
- Secure Business Assets
- Transfer, Manage, or Dissolve Business
- Cancel Subscription Services and Automatic Withdrawals
- Review and Manage Digital Assets
- File all required Tax Returns
- Pay all Outstanding Debts and Taxes
- Liquidate, Bequeath, or Transfer Assets
- Obtain a Clearance Certificate
- Obtain Beneficiary Releases
- Prepare Statement of Executor's Expenses Form
- Prepare Financial Statement Summary Form
- Pay Final Expenses, Professional Fees, Executor's Compensation, and Distributions
- Close Estate Bank Account
- Store Estate Records for Seven (7) Years

Statement of Accounts

List of Assets

The following are samples of *The Empowered Executor's* **List of Assets** forms.

To download the free, printable full forms, visit *https://www.shelleyessery.com*.

Inventory of Assets at Date of Death: ___________________________

Estate of: ____

ASSET	DETAILS	QTY	FMV	SALE PRICE	NOTES

Individual Asset: ____

Estate of: ____

DATE	INCOME	EXPENSE	BALANCE / VALUE	NOTES

Bank or Financial Account: ____

Estate of: ____

DATE	DEPOSIT (CREDIT)	PAYMENT (DEBIT)	DESCRIPTION	BALANCE

Individual Asset: ____

Estate of: ____

DATE	INCOME	EXPENSE	BALANCE / VALUE	NOTES

Bank or Financial Account: ____

Estate of: ____

DATE	DEPOSIT (CREDIT)	PAYMENT (DEBIT)	DESCRIPTION	BALANCE

List of Debts & Liabilities

The following are samples of *The Empowered Executor's* **List of Debts & Liabilities** forms.

To download the free, printable full forms, visit *https://www.shelleyessery.com*.

Debts & Liabilities at Date of Death: _______________________________

Estate of: ____

DEBT / LIABILITY	ACCOUNT #	CREDITOR	AMOUNT O/S	SETTLED

Individual Debt / Liability: ____

Estate of: ____

DATE	INCOME	EXPENSE	BALANCE / VALUE	NOTES

Executor Expenses & Compensation

The following are samples of *The Empowered Executor's* **Executor Expenses & Compensation** forms.

To download the free, printable full forms, visit *https://www.shelleyessery.com*.

Executor's Expense and Compensation Log

Estate of: ____

DATE	EXECUTOR'S EXPENSE	EXECUTOR'S COMPENSATION	AMOUNT	REIMBURSED / PAID

Executor's Time Log

Estate of: ____

DATE	ACTIVITY	HOURS

Financial Statement Summary

The following are samples of *The Empowered Executor's* **Financial Statement Summary** forms.

To download the free, printable full forms, visit *https://www.shelleyessery.com*.

General Cash Flow Worksheet

Estate of: ____

DATE	ACCOUNT	EXPENSE	RECEIPT	AMOUNT	BALANCE

Asset & Liability Financial Summary

Estate of: ____

DATE	ASSET	AMOUNT	BALANCE

DATE	LIABILITY	AMOUNT	BALANCE

DATE	ANTICIPATED INCOME	AMOUNT	BALANCE

DATE	ANTICIPATED EXPENSE	AMOUNT	BALANCE

DATE	EXECUTOR'S EXPENSES & COMPENSATION	AMOUNT	BALANCE

DATE	PROPOSED DISTRIBUTION	AMOUNT	BALANCE

Assets Not Subject to Probate

Estate of: ____

DATE	ASSET	VALUE	DISPOSITION

Executor's Task List & Planner

The following are samples of *The Empowered Executor's* **Executor's Task List & Planner**.

To download the free, printable full forms, visit *https://www.shelleyessery.com*.

PLANNER

DUE DATE	TASK

DUE DATE	TASK

PLANNER

DUE DATE	TASK

PLANNER

DUE DATE	TASK

PLANNER

DUE DATE	TASK

Executor Care & Compassion

As you step into the role of executor, it's essential to remember to care for your health and emotional well-being.

Administering a loved one's estate is a deeply emotional and often exhausting responsibility. Recognizing this early on allows you to incorporate a plan for self-care and compassion into your administration process.

Remember that you are grieving, and that grief does not operate on a schedule. You can't control when and how it will affect you. That's why taking care of yourself throughout this process, both physically and emotionally, is so important.

When stress builds, it's natural to push your own needs aside. However, having a plan to support your well-being can provide comfort when you're navigating the dual challenges of administering an estate and grieving a loved one.

The best approach is often the simplest: be gentle with yourself. Prioritize nourishing foods, stay hydrated, engage in some physical activity, and make sure you're getting enough rest.

Spending time in nature is another great way to help decrease anxiety and stress. Nature has been shown to have a positive affect on both our physical and mental health.

Use the questions on the following pages to create a plan for your self-care. These prompts can also serve as a quick reference to support your well-being throughout your executor journey.

Nutrition

What are some of your favourite nutritious foods?
What are some of your favourite healthy recipes?
What is your favourite non-alcoholic beverage?
What is your favourite comfort food?
What is your favourite treat?
What is your favourite home-cooked meal?
What is your favourite restaurant?
What is your favourite coffeehouse?

Physical Activity

What is your favourite form of physical movement?
What is your favourite sport?
Where is your favourite place to go for a walk?
Where is your favourite bike trail?
What is your favourite social physical activity?
Where is your favourite park or beach?

____

____

____

____

____

____

____

____

____

____

Sleep

What is your natural sleep schedule?
How many hours of sleep do you typically need?
What is your favourite bedtime routine?
What helps you unwind?
Do you like to nap?

Introspection

What is your favourite way to enjoy being around water?
Do you like going to the beach, taking a long, hot shower, or soaking in a bubble bath?
Do you enjoy reading?
Do you enjoy journalling?
What is your favourite creative outlet?
Do you practice mindfulness or meditation?
Where is your "thinking place"?

____

____

____

____

____

____

____

____

____

Social Connections

Who makes up your support system?
Who do you have the most fun with?
Who do you have the most heart-to-heart
conversations with?
Who is your safe person when you feel vulnerable?
Do you have a favourite group activity?

____

____

____

____

____

____

____

____

____

____

Connect with Nature

Do you enjoy going for walks?
Do you enjoy gardening?
Do you enjoy going to the beach?
Do you enjoy listening to the rain?
Do you enjoy birdwatching?
Do you enjoy the feeling of sunshine on your skin?

Grief Support

Dealing with grief is a deeply personal process. There is no timeline with grief and no way of knowing when it will hit you. Try to be patient with yourself and understand that it's okay to have good days and bad days.

Below are some strategies you might find helpful as you navigate the process:

1. Allow Yourself to Grieve. It's important to acknowledge your feelings, whether it's sadness, anger, or confusion. Grief is a natural response to loss.

2. Seek Support. Talk to friends, family, or a therapist. Sharing your feelings can be incredibly healing. There are also many support groups where you can connect with others who are going through similar experiences.

3. Take Care of Yourself. Grief can be physically exhausting. Make sure you're eating well, getting enough sleep, and taking time for yourself.

4. Practice Rituals. Light a candle, visit a special place, or create a memory book.

5. Express Your Emotions. Start a journal, create art, or engage in other forms of creative expression to help you process your emotions.

6. Remember the Person. Find ways to honour and remember the person you've lost.

Grief is a journey, and there's no right or wrong way to work through it. The key is to be kind to yourself and allow yourself to feel whatever emotions come up without judgment, quilt, or shame.

Questions &
Concerns

Executor's Questions & Concerns

Will Maker's Questions & Concerns

Family's Questions & Concerns

Uncomfortable Conversations

Being an intended executor for someone who is hesitant about discussing their end of life wishes can be particularly challenging. The goal is to let your loved one know that you're asking these questions out of love and a desire to honour their wishes.

Asking about their wishes for their estate after they've passed is a sensitive, but important conversation. It's one you'll have to approach with care. If having an in-person discussion is too uncomfortable or just isn't an option, consider asking questions digitally (via email, for example), through a shared physical or digital notebook, or through a third party who does not hold an interest in the estate.

You can even share this guide with them and ask them to fill in their personal information, leave any notes on the will maker's questions & concerns page, or use these prompts however feels comfortable to them. This can provide a buffer for a more comfortable discussion and allow each of you to share your concerns, ask questions, and receive the answers you need in a more comfortable, non confrontational setting.

Below are some prompts to guide you through these conversations. These are suggestions only, and I encourage you to paraphrase them using your own words:

"I know this might be a tough topic, but I want to make sure we're prepared. What are some things you'd like us to consider for your estate and memorial arrangements?"

"Have you thought about who you'd like to manage your estate after you're gone? It would be helpful to know your preferences so we can ensure things go smoothly for the family."

"Do you have a will or other testamentary documents? Where are they kept? It would give me peace of mind to know everything is in place."

"Are there any items — family heirlooms, photos, or personal belongings — that you'd like to be given to specific people? I want to make sure your wishes are honoured."

"Is there anything sentimental you'd want us to hold onto or distribute in a particular way? I'd love to make sure we respect that."

"Have you thought about what kind of memorial or service you'd like? We want to celebrate your life in the way that feels right to you."

"Do you have any preferences for how you'd like to be remembered — whether it's with a memorial or another type of gathering?"

"What values or traditions would you like us to carry forward? Your guidance would help us honor you in a meaningful way."

"Is there a message or specific memory you'd want to pass on to the family?

*Something you'd like future generations
to know?"*

*"Is there someone specific you trust to handle
things, or would you prefer we share
responsibilities in certain ways?"*

*"Would you feel comfortable discussing how we
could best support each other as a family after
you're gone?"*

*"What would you like us to do with your home or
any other significant assets? How can we make
sure we're making the right decisions?"*

*"I know it's tough to think about, but are there
any health or medical decisions you'd want us to
know about if you're unable to tell us?"*

*"How can we best support you as you age? Is there
anything you'd want us to keep in mind when the
time comes?"*

Additional Services

<u>**Executor Support - The Empowered Executor**</u>

Whether you're looking for detailed guidance or just some reassurance along the way, I'm here to support you in getting organized and confidently managing an estate. For personalized assistance and more in-depth executor support, email *connect@shelleyessery.com*.

To download full versions of the sample forms included in this guide, go to https://www.shelleyessery.com

Additional Services

<u>Estate Organizing and Planning -The Empowered Estate and More</u>

The Empowered Estate is your all-in-one binder designed to keep your most important information organized and accessible. From emergency contacts and vital stats to your list of assets, banking details, pet care, end-of-life plans, and even your legacy work - it's all included, neatly tucked into one comprehensive binder, which comes complete with an engaging and interactive workshop to make sure you are fully supported.

PLUS - introducing The Empowered Family, designed to facilitate open conversations, and provide guidance & resources to help families express and discuss their values and preferences.

For more information, email *connect@theempoweredestate.ca.*

Additional Services

<u>**Custom Memorial Engraving -** *For Love Engraving*</u>

During times of loss, memories are the most cherished possessions we have. They are the comforting whispers of loved ones, the shared laughter, and the echoes of moments that touched our hearts. For Love Engraving can help you honour and remember those you hold dear in a way that truly reflects your special bond.

Design a unique and personalized memorial keepsake to beautifully embody the spirit of your beloved. This special item could feature a heartfelt message, a cherished image, or a one-of-a-kind design that truly honours their memory.

Our services also extend to pay tribute to the beloved pets who have brought immeasurable joy and unconditional love into your life.

For help lovingly preserving the life and legacy of your loved one, email *sales@forloveengraving.com* or connect at *www.forloveengraving.com*.

About the Author

Shelley Essery is a serial entrepreneur, author, and former Wills & Estates and Real Estate Legal Administrator helping families navigate the often-overwhelming world of estate administration. As Co-Founder of The Empowered Estate, Shelley is passionate about helping individuals take a proactive approach to end-of-life planning, and ensuring peace of mind for both will makers & their families. Her unique perspective serves to bridge the gap between executors, will makers, and grieving families, ensuring a holistic and compassionate approach to estate administration.

With a blend of legal experience and empathy, Shelley's work prioritizes the importance of maintaining healthy relationships throughout the process. *The Executor's Survival Guide – A Holistic Approach for Canadian Families* addresses the needs of executors while fostering a deeper understanding of the interconnected roles between will makers, executors, & the deceased's loved ones alike, and reflects Shelley's commitment to supporting all involved during one of life's most challenging times.